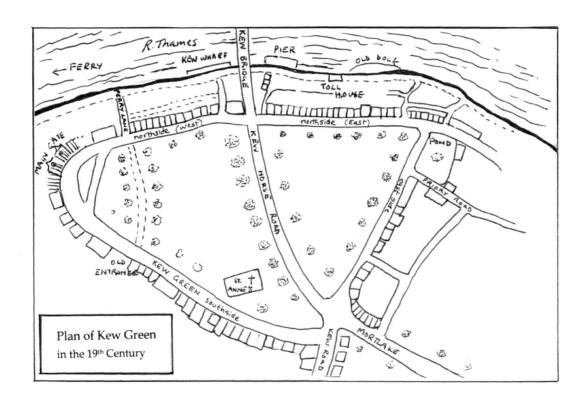

R.Thames

← FERRY

KEW WHARF

FERRY LANE

KEW BRIDGE

PIER

OLD DOCK

TOLL HOUSE

northside (West)

northside (East)

MAIN GATE

KEW HORSE ROAD

POND

PRIORY ROAD

KEW ROAD

OLD ENTRANCE

KEW GREEN Southside

ST. ANNE'S

MORTLAKE

KEW ROAD

Plan of Kew Green
in the 19th Century

2

KEW GREEN ILLUSTRATED

ANNE ABERCROMBIE

Published by Kew Lane Publications, 100 Mortlake Road, Kew TW9 4AS

Text and Illustrations © Anne Abercrombie 2012

ISBN   978-0-9574952-0-3

Typeface :   Palatino Linotype

Printed by Short Run Press Ltd

This little book about the growth of Kew Green in the 19th Century should be regarded as a collection and assimilation of material gathered from other people's research and from material in the public domain, such as census records and trade directories. However, I hope the overview it gives will prove interesting and perhaps add something to earlier interpretations. The Royal family's residence in Kew clearly influenced Kew Green's development, but it is the increase in the variety of skills and talents of the local community which has been so interesting to discover.

I have concentrated on events between 1840 and the 1890s, with reference to the origins of the buildings round Kew Green. We have an amazing amount of material in the National Archives in Kew and the staff there have been extremely helpful. We also have erudite local historians on whose scholarship I have relied heavily. I particularly thank David Blomfield for encouraging this non-historian in her endeavours, and John Cloake for his research into Kew Green's development. The Richmond Local Studies department staff have also been very helpful.

Finally, my family deserve many thanks for their patience, support, suggestions and help.

For centuries people came upriver from London to enjoy the clean air and the great open spaces in which to ride. Often they stopped at Kew, but this little hamlet began to grow in popularity when monarchs brought their courtiers with them, and established their large houses.

The earliest buildings on the Green were not, in fact, mansions but cottages. The earliest recorded grants for these were given by Queen Elizabeth I in the late 16th Century when the Green covered a much greater area. These buildings became numbers 1 to 15 Kew Green.

Other grants were given and cottages built, mostly on the south side of the Green. These grants are recorded in the Manor Rolls and have been diligently researched by John Cloake. They are detailed in his book, *Cottages and Common Fields of Richmond*.

If, today, when walking across Kew Green towards the Gardens, you can ignore the buzz of traffic, the sirens of emergency vehicles and the planes overhead, then you can quite easily imagine yourself being in this same place a hundred and fifty years or so ago.

The buildings which surround the Green have changed little in that time. Some are as they were built in the 18th Century. Most remain as family homes but some have been divided into flats while the smaller cottages on the east side have been extended.

Tea rooms and hotels have come and gone and some shops have been converted into houses, while others are now restaurants. However, over all the years the loveliness and freedom which this open space affords have remained.

Where animals once grazed, children now fly kites, kick footballs and run with their dogs – and people of all ages play cricket.

We know from the 1838 Directory of Surrey, where Kew is entered under the Richmond Union, that the Posting House for Kew was then at the King's Arms by the Bridge, and run by Samuel Taylor but the 1841 census shows that Henry Taylor, a baker living at number 3 Kew Green, had incorporated a Post Office into his baker's shop and that he had become the postmaster. By 1878 the premises are described as 'Post, Money Order and Telegraph Office and Savings Bank', with Henry Taylor still the Postmaster. Interestingly, this Post Office Directory also states that:

"Letters arrive from London at 7 & 8.30am; 2.20, 6.30 & 8.30pm and are despatched at 9.40am, 12.40. 4.45 & 8.30pm: Sundays arriving at 9.40am and being despatched at 9.10pm."

In 1929 Richmond Council compulsorily purchased numbers 1 to 7 Kew Green in order to widen Kew Road. The buildings were bulldozed and Kelland's became the corner shop. This drawing, based on a photograph taken in 1910, shows the row of cottages 1 to 7, with shops on the ground floor and accommodation above.

Numbers 1 to 7 Kew Green

The Botanist

After the road widening the buildings on Kew Green were renumbered with those on the west side being given odd numbers and those on the east side, even numbers. Kelland's, the butcher's shop, became number 9. When it ceased to be a butcher's it became Jasper's Bun in the Oven. It was adapted but retained most of its earlier features. The wide entrance, which had allowed animals and carts to pass through to the yard at the back, is still there with its heavy oak doors. The large butcher's window has also been kept, as have the blue and white ceramic tiles below it. The business has changed hands several times since but it has remained an eating place, as Pissarro's, named after the painter who once lived nearby and painted this view of Kew Green, then Brown's, and more recently The Botanist, now with its own micro-brewery.

Numbers 9 to 15 housed the Layton family's Rising Sun tavern, probably at number 11. Mary Layton became the licensee and in 1700 her son inherited the business. William Gainforth then became the landlord and by 1763 had changed the name to the Coach and Horses. By 1770 the inn had moved across the road to much larger premises on the east side. The old cottages, rebuilt in the 1830s, have housed butchers, confectioners, a bookseller, an antiques dealer, and a tobacconist, among others.

The row of houses, 17 to 25 Kew Green, is shown as Cambridge Terrace in the census of 1891. The first buildings were erected in the late 1620s but rebuilt in the mid-18th Century. The painter Gainsborough moved to London in 1774 and stayed here for some time. He painted a famous portrait of King George III and Queen Charlotte in 1781 and when he died in 1788, was buried in St. Anne's churchyard.

The botanical illustrator Franz Bauer lived at number 23 from 1804 to 1837.

Numbers 29 and 31 are 18th Century houses, number 27 having been added later.

Walter Hood Fitch, another brilliant botanical artist who worked at Kew Gardens, lived in several different houses in the village, finally moving with his family to number 31, Llewellyn House where he died in 1892. In his lifetime he produced more than twelve thousand illustrations, many for Curtis's Botanical Magazine, as well as his prolific output of work for Kew.

Numbers 17 to 25, Cambridge Terrace

Number 27   Charlton House   Llewellyn House

14

King's Cottage and King's Lodge

Number 33, King's Cottage, was leased to Lord Bute in 1758. He lived at number 37 but used 33 as a study and a place in which to house his large botanical library and Herbarium. As well as being a politician and becoming Prime Minister in 1762, he was an enthusiastic and knowledgeable botanist.

Number 35 is King's Lodge.

In 1773 this group of houses was bought by the King, George III, for his family.

Number 33 was given to the Duke of Cumberland and when he moved across the Green it became Church House. However, the census returns show no vicar having lived there between 1841 and 1861. On the 1896 Ordnance Survey map it is marked as Church House, perhaps simply because it is opposite the Church.

Numbers 37 to 45 were given to the Duke of Cambridge.

He enlarged Cambridge Cottage in 1838 and added the porch in 1840. He died in 1850 and the Duchess lived there for the rest of her life. After the death of her surviving son in 1904, the building became the Forestry Museum in Kew Gardens.

The Gables, with their Dutch-inspired architecture, were built in the 1730s. The oldest part was used as stabling for Cambridge Cottage. Later the area became the yard of the Office of Works. In 1908 it was rebuilt as housing for members of Kew Gardens staff.

Number 37. Cambridge Cottage

The Gables

The site of number 47 was granted in 1578 and there was a cottage here by 1579. The house was owned by the Capel family in 1680. In 1697 Lady Dorothy Capel was granted a licence to let the property for twenty-one years. Elizabeth Nixon took the lease and became the licensed victualler of the Rose and Crown. After her death a new lease was given to her son, Arthur Nixon in 1711. It was subsequently passed to John Hayter who then sub-let it to a Richmond schoolmaster, James Smith. In 1729 the Rose and Crown moved to one of three cottages at number 79 on the north side of the Green. By 1774 it occupied all three cottages.

Meanwhile, number 47 was used as a school, 'Hell House', later as a barracks and then as a Fire House until 1908. After 1945 it was rebuilt and is now the Administration Offices of Kew Gardens.

It was here that the first main entrance to the Gardens was built, now marked by an engraved slate plaque on the right-hand gatepost.

Number 47

Number 49, The Director's House

Numbers 49 and 51 Kew Green replaced an earlier house, known to have existed in 1603. It was sold 'with seven and a half acres', demolished and rebuilt by J.Schennerstadt in about 1758. When Sir William Hooker became the first Director of the Royal Botanic Gardens in 1841, he left West Park and moved to number 49 Kew Green. His son, Sir Joseph Hooker, followed him as Director in 1865 and he too lived there. Since then this has been the home of each Director during his time in office.

Number 51, a Grace and Favour house, is known as Royal Cottage.

Number 53 was occupied by John Smith, the Curator of Kew Gardens from 1841 to 1868. It is known as the Curator's House.

Number 55 is where the Duke of Cambridge lived as a boy and where Joseph Hooker lived for a while. He enlarged it in 1855 and it became the home of the Keeper of the Herbarium.

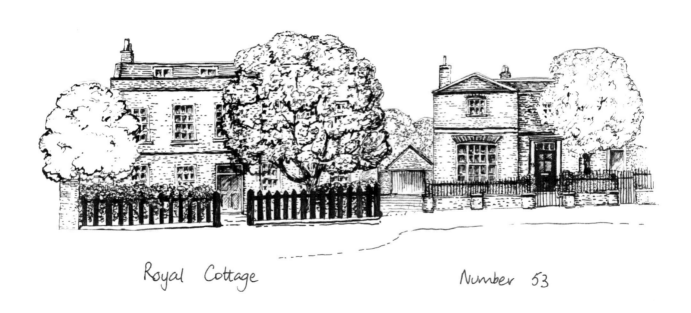

Royal Cottage

Number 53

Number 55

At this point Kew Green curves round to the north following the shape of the present main entrance to the Gardens. The first gates, erected in about 1825, were at number 47. They had been supported on each side by a square lodge, one surmounted by a carved stone lion, the other by a unicorn. These sculptures were moved when the entrance was re-sited, but can still be seen. The lion sits on top of the Lion Gate entrance in Kew Road while the unicorn lies above a doorway on Kew Road near to the Victoria Gate.

The new Main Gates are supported by elegant stone pillars surmounted by decorative urns, and form the centrepiece of Decimus Burton's design for the semi-circular entrance.

Burton was also the architect of the Temperate House and, with the engineer Richard Turner, designed the Palm House in the Gardens.

The building we know today as Kew Palace is inside the Gardens near to the Main Gate. It was built in the 1630s and was known as the Dutch House because of its Dutch-influenced architecture. It replaced an earlier building, the cellars and kitchens of which have been discovered under Kew Palace. At the moment there is some debate as to the origins of that house. The first Kew Palace stood just to the south of the Dutch House. Old prints show it to have been a long, low, white building, hence its name, the White House. It was demolished in 1802 and the Royal family moved across the lawn to the red-bricked Dutch House.

The present Kew Palace was first opened to the public in 1899. Toys with which the children had played were exhibited, among them ivory discs each little more than an inch in diameter, engraved with the letters of the alphabet on one side and a picture of a corresponding subject on the other: the forerunner of flash cards, perhaps? Another exhibit of note was shown in a half-cupboard on the landing in which were displayed some of King George's wigs. The Palace and its kitchens, having been restored, are now open to the public again.

Number 57, The Herbarium

Number 57 Kew Green houses the Herbarium of the Royal Botanic Gardens.

The grant for the building of two cottages on this land was given by Elizabeth I. The house which later replaced them was itself demolished by the 1650s and two new houses built on the site. In one, Sir Peter Lely is known to have lived. The other was called Hunter House after its owner in 1800, Robert Hunter. Then in 1820, after the site was bought by the King, it was known as Hanover House, until the Herbarium was established in 1852 and it became Herbarium House.

Jeremiah Meyer is believed to have lived in the other house on the site. He was employed by the King as 'Painter in Miniatures and Enamels'. Meyer was also a founder member of the Royal Academy. He died in 1789 and is buried in St. Anne's churchyard.

After Meyer's death the little lane beside Hanover House was renamed Meyer's Lane. It later became Ferry Lane.

The sites of 59 and 61 had been granted by Queen Elizabeth, with a cottage built by 1635, then rebuilt at different times as one house, or in some cases as two houses. Today there is no number 59 Kew Green. The 1861 census numbers two separate addresses on the Herbarium site, but since the numbering system differs from one census to another it can be difficult to determine precisely where 59 was. Number 61, Abingdon House was a girls' boarding school in 1851 and in 1891, as Ebor House, recorded as a Ladies' School. It is now Abingdon House once more.

Number 63 was similarly a building replacing an earlier cottage. In 1861 the head of the household was Letitia Hill, "Lady", who shared her home with her two similarly entitled sisters, all born in Snailwell, a Cambridgeshire village near Newmarket. That must account for the house's name, Snailwell. Years later a serious fire destroyed much of the house, and it was renamed The Dieudonne after being rebuilt. In the 1920s both these houses were bought by Will Evans who established the Imperial Restaurant at number 61 and Tea Rooms at number 63.

Abingdon   La Dieudonne

31

Warden House White House Ada Villa

32

Number 65 Warden House, and number 67 White House, were both built in 1716 as the original buildings on the site. Both houses were altered in the early 19th Century and both later became restaurants: number 65 from 1906 to the 1920s; number 67 from 1906 to the 1930s.

Numbers 69 to 73 were cottages by 1625 and were rebuilt in the late 18th Century when 69 Ada Villa, and 71 Ivy House became one house. They were soon to be divided into three houses in 1804 and then reverted to being two by the 1840s.

Number 73 is called Danebury.

Numbers 75 and 77 Kew Green were granted in 1641.

The site of 75, Carlton House, was stables in the 1750s but rebuilt for F.W. Bush in the 1850s. He is recorded in the 1861 census as a Barrister, Head of the household, living with his wife and five children, and a staff of four.

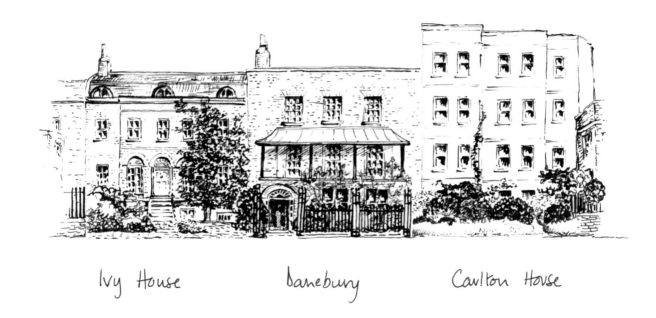

Ivy House   Danebury   Carlton House

Beaconsfield

The Rose and Crown

Number 77 Beaconsfield, may well be the oldest house on Kew Green. The deep, rich colour of its bricks has led to its sometimes being called 'The Red House'. It was bought by Ann Engleheart in 1749. She and her husband Francis lived there until they leased it to Fred Albert, page to Queen Charlotte and father of Mrs. Papendiek, also a Courtier to the Queen. She is remembered for her memoirs of life at Court, with somewhat lively descriptions of the Royal family's life and that of their guests. Clementine Schnell lived in the house until it reverted to the ownership of the Engleheart family in 1842.

The Englehearts were master plasterers who produced intricate decorative ceilings of very high quality for several houses on the Green, number 77 being one example.

Number 79 Kew Green is the Rose and Crown. Having moved from its earlier situation at number 47 on the south side of the Green, it expanded as its popularity grew. It was rebuilt in the 1930s in the mock-Elizabethan style fashionable at the time.

The sites of numbers 81 to 83 were granted in 1671 and by 1712 two cottages had been built. The censuses of 1861 and 1871 describe number 81 as Flora Cottage 48 Kew Green, and 49 Kew Green as Pamona Cottage. We know that Flora House was built in the 1880s, so it presumably replaced both Flora and Pamona Cottages, neither of which appears in the 1891 census. From 1887 Flora House was occupied by William Pring, landlord of the King's Arms, and his family. It was then bought by Will Evans who lived there for the rest of his life.

Number 83, Capel House dates from the early 18th Century. It is not thought to have any connection with the Capel family.

The road which runs from this part of the Green to the river, now called Bush Road, was formerly known as Wharf Road. Several of the watermen, boatbuilders, bargemen and lightermen of Kew lived there. The coal merchants and corn merchants were based at the Wharf. The areas called Cold Harbour and Riverside are nearby, towards the Old Dock.

Flora House   Capel House   Wharf Road

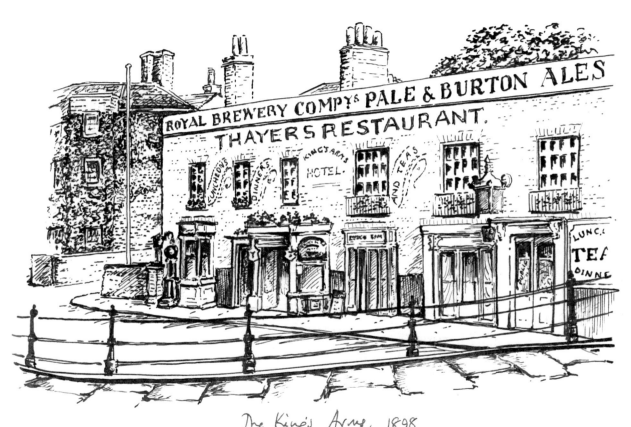

The King's Arms, 1898

The King's Arms   1910

40

The site for number 85 Kew Green was granted in 1701 but it remained open land until after the first bridge had been built. G. Schennerstadt, the owner of the land, then built The King's Arms. It was opened in the 1780s. However, that building had to be demolished for the second bridge to be built. The new building was much larger and more impressive, as the photograph, taken in about 1898, and on which this drawing is based, shows. Unfortunately, it and numbers 87 and 89 had to be pulled down before the third bridge could be built.

Neither the offices of builders Warden and Pring at number 87, nor Miss Pring's tea house and sweetshop at number 89, was rebuilt, but the King's Arms was, in about 1910. It is no longer a public house but has become a restaurant.

The Kew Bridges

It is said that at low tide in times past, it was possible to walk across the river from Kew to Brentford. However, to provide a more reliable journey a ferry went from the Kew bank near what is now called Ferry Lane, to the Middlesex bank near the outlet of what is now the Grand Union Canal.

In 1758/9 a bridge was built by Robert Tunstall, the owner of the ferry. It had eleven arches, two of stone at each bank and seven timber arches between. It was paid for by levying a toll on each pedestrian using the bridge, and a more expensive toll on each horse. In 1774 there was a collision on the river which badly damaged the central arches, and took two years to repair. In 1782 more repairs were needed and so Robert Tunstall (junior) sought plans for a new bridge. James Paine's design for a bridge with nine arches was chosen. He had designed the new, stone Richmond Bridge. The new Kew Bridge took six years to build and was opened by the King, George III in 1789.

The second bridge proved to be very popular, making it much easier for traders to operate. The population was increasing. In 1801 the total population of Kew was 895, by 1841 it had grown to 1,497 and by 1891 reached 4,561. This very large rise can be related to Kew Gardens Station having been built in 1869, allowing trains from London to Richmond to stop at Kew. The roads near to the Green and the station were soon lined with new imposing family houses and the better transport links meant that people could live in Kew and work in London.

The bridge helped the market gardeners taking their produce to Covent Garden, but with success came the problem of congestion. The gradient of the road was too steep and became increasingly dangerous since the bridge was now too narrow for the volume of traffic, so a third bridge was planned, to be built of granite with three arches. It was finally opened by King Edward VII in 1903.

It will have become apparent that the buildings on the west side of the Green owe a great deal to the patronage of King George III and Queen Charlotte. Their enthusiasm, influence and wealth led to the Gardens being developed and opened to the public. Having the monarch living in Kew Palace brought many visitors to the Court. The large houses built for the Royal household needed to be maintained, so they offered employment to local people.

The staff must have been well-treated, since looking through the census returns for different years the same names recur. One in particular, being that of Mary Murphy, a 65 year-old female servant, and later entered as "90 years old and Housekeeper at Kew Palace".

On the north east of the Green there is a much greater variety of buildings. Some cottages appear much as when they were built. The oldest houses date from the1700s, the rest mostly from the 19th Century. Waterloo Place was built between 1814 and 1816.

This area was a hive of activity. There was a variety of shops, while the inhabitants of the cottages followed many different occupations which are clearly recorded on some of the census returns. The commercial section of the Kew Directories of the time lists the different trades which were practised and the names of the owners of the businesses. Interestingly, there were three different coal merchants and four publicans among these traders, all living and working on or very near the Green.

What is more surprising is the number of laundresses, six, living in Waterloo Place and Cold Harbour. It is noticeable too, that this work was carried out by different generations of the same family. Kew had much to thank the Bass family for in providing it with clean linen.

Equally, many of the men of the Williams family were watermen or boat builders over several generations and during all of the period of this study. Other families, most notably the Taylors, Prings, Costelows, Humphreys and Laytons among them, established themselves in Kew over many years in a variety of trades.

Until it had to be demolished in 1900 for the building of the third bridge, the blacksmith's shop was the first building on the north east side of Kew Green. It is recorded as being a working forge by 1777. In 1841 Mark Hutson was the farrier. A photograph was taken in 1900 and it is on this that the drawing of the building is based.

The building next to the blacksmith's must have been the butcher, Robert Surman's shop. The 1841 census states that Robert Surman, butcher, aged 45, lived there. In 1851 its occupants are still the Surmans and the census indicates them living next door to the farrier. Even the building itself suggests it was a butcher's, with its wide entrance similar to that of Kelland's on the south side of the Green. In the recent past the building housed the Caxton Name Plate Manufacturing Company. Its name is still attached to the west wall. However, this building has another claim to fame. At the back of it there is a small hut-shaped extension. It is passed by anyone going to Westerly Ware, but nothing about it attracts any attention today. It used to be the mortuary where bodies which had washed up on the riverbank were kept before they were taken for identification.

The Farrier's Shop 1900

Cottages, Waterloo Place

Waterloo Place

The sites for the cottages on the north east of the Green were granted in 1741. The next ten cottages in Waterloo Place were built in 1814, the other nine in 1816. The Greyhound public house was recorded as being an inn in 1850, though it was later rebuilt. Myrtle Cottage dates from 1820. A photograph taken from the Pond in about 1900 shows that the east-facing wall of this building was plain, without the windows or the front door which are there today and were clearly added later. A narrow road past this east side of the house leads to the back of Waterloo Place, Willow Cottages and, in the opposite direction, to Cambridge Cottages.

Waterloo Place

Waterloo Place   Myrtle Cottage

Waterloo Place, 1900s

These houses, with those in neighbouring Willow Cottages and Thetis Terrace, also date from the 1860s. The first three cottages facing the Pond are of a similar vintage, then there is a modern building where for many years there was a builder's yard. Beside it stand three cottages built of deep red brick. Originally these made up a row of four, but the one on the corner, Hawarden Cottage, was demolished in the late 1940s. They were known as Pond cottages and they date from 1726. Today they are Rose Cottage, Home Cottage, and Pond Cottage. One of them is recorded as having been an alehouse known as the 'Peterboat'. The first licensee was probably John Manger, the second, Ralph Cheshire.

Kew Pond

Kew Pond is an attractive feature of the Green. It is fringed with bulrushes and water irises which make it particularly lovely in the spring. It has an island in the middle where moorhens, mallards and swans all make nests and, when their young are hatched, give yet more pleasure to people passing. Herons too are among the regular visitors to the Pond.

In earlier times it was not simply there to enhance the neighbourhood, but met practical needs as well. It was thought to have been a fish pond – for fish to be caught and sold, since at that time the river was rich in fish. The water level in the Pond changed with the tide on the river, since a waterway linked the two. This man-made inlet was wide enough for the King's Barge to be moored there. The ramp at the Pond's north west corner is where horses could be led to drink and where drivers could soak the wheels of their carts to tighten them against their metal rims.

On the north side of the Pond is a row of modern houses. These were built on the site of the old Queen's School, after it moved to Cumberland Road in 1970.

Bradfield Gardens and Kew Pond

Nearby, in what was Bradfield Gardens, stands a row of four distinctive houses facing the Pond. They are built of red brick with decorative white stonework.

To the south of the Pond is the large area of land on which the Priory stood. It was bought in 1810 by Miss Doughty, a wealthy woman from Richmond. It is on this land that the roads leading from the east side of the Green were built.

The impressive row of six three-storey houses facing the Green was known as Priory Terrace and built between 1871 and 1891, when it appears on the census.

Priory Terrace

Dunedin   Haverfield House   East Side

Number 26 Kew Green is called Dunedin, number 24 Haverfield House, and number 22 East Side. Number 20 was earlier known as Mason's House and is now called Sedburgh. It may well be the original 1720s house. The colour of the bricks alone suggests this. The age of the present house at number 18, Hope House, is more debatable as it is covered in stucco, hiding the bricks, so it may have been rebuilt in the 19th Century.

Numbers 16, 14, 12 and 10 make up the row called Gloucester Terrace. These were four houses in 1773, reduced to two by 1810.

In the 1720s the Cock and Hoop tavern was in one of the buildings, becoming the Ewe and Lamb in the 1730s.

Number 16 was Hope Cottage and number 10 Kew Cottage.

By 1841 they were four houses again, number 10 being the Royal Standard tavern.

They all became shops in the early 20th Century.

Mason's House

Hope House

Gloucester Terrace

Number 8 the Coach and Horses Inn, having moved from the south side of the Green in 1771, established itself as a well-run coaching inn. Its position on the Kew Horse Road linking Richmond and Kew with the main road to London brought plenty of passing trade as well as people wishing to stay overnight.

It remains a popular inn, well-supported by the local population and its many visitors.

The Coach and Horses

The Stables

Behind the inn are stables, so it would seem reasonable to think they were part of the inn's premises. No one seems able to confirm this, nor whether they belonged to Richmond House, or even if they were perhaps one of a group of stables which existed on this land before they were demolished to make way for the building of Mortlake Terrace in the 1870s.

Stables are clearly marked here on early 19th Century maps.

Number 6 Victoria Cottage, on the far left of the drawing opposite, is an unusual building dating from 1840 when it was squeezed between the inn and Richmond House, and became the office of a house agent.

The site for numbers 2 to 4 Kew Green, now Richmond House, was granted in 1635 and there was a cottage here by 1658. It was rebuilt and adapted at various times, but was bought in its present state by the Duke of Cumberland in 1804-6. He used it as accommodation for soldiers.

In the 1890s it was the London and Provincial Bank and then Barclay's Bank, until it closed in the 1970s. Since then it has been a shop and flats.

Victoria Cottage   Richmond House

69

Mortlake Terrace

Mortlake Terrace is not actually on Kew Green but it is an imposing and significant row of shops very nearby. The Terrace, completed by 1876, is on an area of land at the west end of Mortlake Road. There are nine shops in the row, with two storeys above. The premises were each let on a twenty-one year repairing lease.

Number 1a Mortlake Terrace was not recorded until 1900. Was it a shop when the row was built, or was it a later addition? If you look at number 1a from the other side of Mortlake Road you may notice that, whereas the top floor windows of 1 to 9 follow the same design, that of 1a is different. The stone dressing under the sill is not continued, and it is not a sash window. The first floor window is also different from that of its neighbour. The roofline too protrudes above the gutters of the rest of the row. The interior of the shop is wedge-shaped, tapering to the back, as though it is filling an existing gap.

It would seem odd to start the numbering at 1a, then 1, 2 and so on. In the past, however, the numbering on Kew Green was not always consistent, as can be seen on census returns.

Number 1a

Looking from Mortlake Terrace across the Green we see the magnificent trees which surround it. They absorb a lot of the pollution from traffic and give a country air to this open space. We also see an iconic building, with a pale turquoise cupola on the clock tower. It is St. Anne's Church, very distinctive and easily recognised.

It began as a small chapel in which local people could worship. It was paid for by donations from local inhabitants, with the generous gift of the site and one hundred pounds from Queen Anne. It has since been enlarged at various times to its present size.

In its churchyard are buried people of national and international fame, but also many who are less well known, and others who appear to be long forgotten. They are all buried here because they had links with Kew, or lived in Kew, and each made his or her contribution to maintaining the friendly atmosphere of this lovely place.

St. Anne's Church

This book began with the drawings of all the buildings on Kew Green. The historical facts have been collected from the following sources, but the interpretations are mine.

The census returns of 1841 to the 1890s

The Directory of Surrey 1838
Robson's Directory 1838
Mason's Directory 1853
Green's Directory 1872/3
Post Office Directory 1878

Planning applications where they exist.

The Story of Kew, and *Kew Past*, both by David Blomfield
Cottages and Common Fields of Richmond and Kew by John Cloake

Much of this material is available online

List of Illustrations